SPOT THE DIFFERENCES

Art Masterpiece Mysteries

BOOK 1

DOVER PUBLICATIONS, INC.
Mineola, New York

Series Concept and Project Editor: Diane Teitel Rubins
Design Concept: Alan Weller
Designer: Joel Waldrep
Senior Editor: Susan L. Rattiner

Copyright

Bibliographical Note

Spot the Differences: Art Masterpiece Mysteries, Book 1 is a new work, first published by Dover Publications, Inc., in 2010.

International Standard Book Number
ISBN-13: 978-0-486-47299-7
ISBN-10: 0-486-47299-X

Manufactured in the United States by Courier Corporation
47299X01
www.doverpublications.com

How well do you truly know the great masterpieces of fine art?

In this book of 25 famous paintings, you will find anywhere from 6 to 14 changes that were made to the originals—from some very obvious differences all the way down to the tiniest little detail. The original painting and the one in which we have made changes are side by side, so you must inspect them both ever so carefully! Just remember: the original work of art always appears on the *left* side! Use your keen observational skills to compare the two pages, and see if you can detect all the differences that appear on the right side of the page. As you discover the differences, remember to keep score by checking the boxes provided on each puzzle page.

Once you have finished strolling through this outstanding gallery of images, you may go to page 54 to check your answers to the puzzles. Try not to peek, though, until you have tried your best to find all the changes! As you go along through the book, you'll learn exciting facts about each painting and its artist. This book is a wonderful and fun introduction to some of the world's greatest works of art.

Ambrosius Bosschaert
Bouquet of Flowers on a Ledge (c. 1618)

Bosschaert often included the same flowers, insects, and shells in his still life paintings.

The paintings by Bosschaert are often regarded as flower portraits, since his work was considered to be so accurate that people compared it to a portrait of someone's face.

All of Bosschaert's children became painters, but none were as famous as their father.

In 1621 Bosschaert died while on his way to deliver one of his floral still life paintings to Prince Maurice of The Hague.

Pieter Bruegel the Elder
Hunters in the Snow (1565)

There's lots of lively activity in this 16th-century wintry painting and, the longer you look at it, the more there is to see. There are tiny houses, churches, horses, wagons, and bridges…plus people hunting, ice fishing, skating, and even cooking outdoors.

In the distance, just underneath the flying bird, there is a house with a chimney fire. In tiny detail, the artist painted people running to the rescue with ladders to help put out the blaze.

Bruegel had two sons, Pieter the Younger and Jan. When both boys grew up to be artists, their father became known as Pieter Bruegel the Elder, to distinguish his paintings from those of his sons.

The artist is known by the nickname "Peasant Bruegel" since he often shows peasants in their everyday lives within his paintings.

Keep Score: 14 Changes ☐ ☐ ☐ ☐ ☐ ☐ ☐ ☐ ☐ ☐ ☐ ☐ ☐ ☐

Gustave Caillebotte
Rue de Paris (1877)

Artist Caillebotte painted exquisite landscapes and portraits, but he is most famous for his scenes of Parisian city life during the 19th century.

Caillebotte painted in a more realistic style than that of his friends, the Impressionist painters Degas, Monet, and Renoir.

The artist's family owned property in the busy neighborhood of the Saint-Lazare train station in Paris.

The artist bought many pictures from other Impressionist painters, and after his death, he left his large collection of art to the French government.

Caillebotte was also a racing yachtsman who had a passion for speed.

Keep Score: 11 Changes ☐ ☐ ☐ ☐ ☐ ☐ ☐ ☐ ☐ ☐ ☐

Vittore Carpaccio
Young Knight in a Landscape (1510)

Known for his scenes of Venice, Carpaccio's paintings are full of lively details of Venetian life.

Although the identity of the young knight in the painting remains a mystery to this day, many art historians believe him to be Francesco Maria della Rovere, III Duke of Urbino. If the painting ever proves to be a portrait, it would be the first known full-length portrait.

On the bottom left, among the plants, is a scroll with the words "MALO MORI QUAM FOEDARI," translated to mean "Better to die than to lose one's honor."

The painting is signed and dated on a small label that is painted as if stuck to a branch at the bottom right of the picture.

Until the 20th century, Carpaccio's signature was painted over and this work was mistakenly credited to Albrecht Dürer.

Keep Score:
14 Changes

☐ ☐ ☐ ☐ ☐
☐ ☐ ☐ ☐ ☐
☐ ☐ ☐ ☐

Mary Cassatt
In the Loge (1878)

This painting was the first of Cassatt's Impressionist paintings to be displayed in the United States.

Mary Cassatt was one of only three women—and the only American—ever to join the French Impressionists, a small group of independent French artists.

Although born in America, Mary spent most of her adult life in Paris.

Mary Cassatt once wrote "Women should be someone and not something."

Most of her early Paris paintings are set in the theater. Cassatt never depicts women onstage or backstage, or, for that matter, anywhere else but in the audience.

The United States Postal Service issued two commemorative stamps in honor of Mary Cassatt. The first, appearing in 1966, was a five-cent stamp picturing her painting, *The Boating Party*, on it. The second, issued in 1988, was a twenty-three-cent stamp of her portrait.

Keep Score:
7 Changes

☐ ☐ ☐ ☐
☐ ☐ ☐

Paul Cézanne
Still Life with Apples (1893–94)

Cézanne believed that everything in the world was made up of a sphere, a cone, a cylinder, or a cube. He began many of his works using these basic shapes.

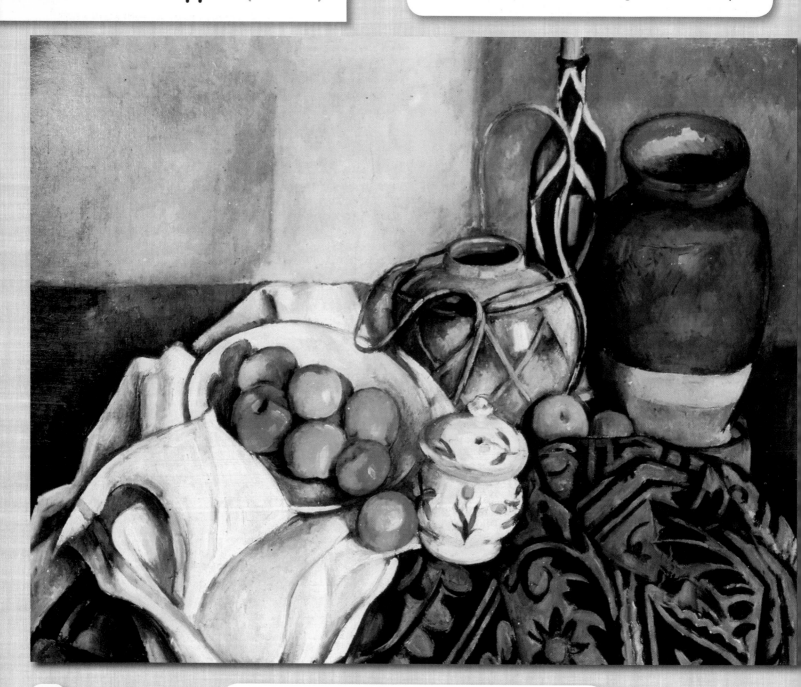

Cézanne is often described as "the Father of Modern Art."

In 2007, one of Cézanne's still life watercolor paintings sold for more than $25 million!

The artist completed more than 200 still life paintings in his lifetime.

Edgar Degas
The Dance Class (1873-76)

Degas is known as the "Painter of Dancers." His unique scenes of ballerinas have become world famous.

In this painting, the dancers in the foreground are not the main focus of attention. Instead, your eye is led diagonally from above, as if you're looking at the scene from the wings of the theater.

In 1873, Degas was among the founding members of the Impressionist group that also included Pissarro, Monet, and Renoir.

Unlike the other Impressionists, Degas preferred workshop painting and never shared their love for the countryside and painting in open-air settings.

Keep Score:
8 Changes

☐ ☐ ☐ ☐
☐ ☐ ☐ ☐

Albrecht Dürer
Self-Portrait (1498)

Albrecht Dürer was born third in a line of 18 children.

Dürer was a painter and engraver as well as an author.

Dürer had a fondness for portraits that began when he was only thirteen years old and completed a pencil self-portrait that showed his considerable talent.

Near the middle of the 15th century, the printing press was invented (until that time, books had been written entirely by hand). Dürer was one of the first artists to take advantage of this new process. By carving illustrations into wood, Dürer made copies of his designs by inking the woodblock and pressing the engraving onto damp paper. Because engravings could easily be carried on horseback, Dürer's fame spread quickly throughout Europe.

Keep Score:

8 Changes

☐ ☐ ☐ ☐
☐ ☐ ☐ ☐

Jan van Eyck
The Arnolfini Portrait
(1434)

Van Eyck is considered one of the best Northern European painters of the 15th century. His contemporaries referred to him as the "King of Painters."

The Latin signature on the wall—"Johannes de Eyck fuit hic 1434"—literally translates to mean "Jan van Eyck was here 1434."

The mirror on the wall reflects two figures in the doorway. One could be van Eyck himself!

Van Eyck became court painter to the Duke of Burgundy and he often traveled on secret missions for him.

Van Eyck's older brother, Hubert, was also a painter and the two brothers would occasionally work together. Sometimes, Jan would finish a painting that his brother had started!

This painting's smooth surface came from applying many layers of paint mixed with oil. It was then covered in varnish. This technique was perfected by van Eyck, and used by many later painters.

Keep Score:
11 Changes

☐ ☐ ☐ ☐
☐ ☐ ☐ ☐
☐ ☐ ☐

Paul Gauguin
The Meal (1891)

This still life painting actually has nothing to do with a real meal, as it is not customary in Tahiti to eat at a table.

Gauguin had a successful career as a stockbroker when he took up painting as a hobby.

A restless man, Gauguin traveled and worked in the French regions of Brittany and Provence as well as the South and Central Americas. In 1891, he moved to the French colony of Tahiti in search of an exotic life in "paradise." He spent all but two of the remaining years of his life in the South Seas.

Original Gauguin paintings are rarely found for sale. If they are, the asking price could be close to $40 million.

Vincent van Gogh
Bedroom in Arles (1889)

This painting depicts Van Gogh's bedroom at Place Lamartine in Arles, Bouches-du-Rhone, France, known as his Yellow House.

Van Gogh sold only one painting in his entire lifetime—*Red Vineyard at Arles* (now in the Pushkin Museum, Moscow).

Van Gogh wrote more than 700 letters to his brother, Theo. The letters, published after his death, provide a written record of the artist's life.

There are three authentic versions of this painting, as described by van Gogh's letters. The way to tell them apart is by the pictures on the painting's wall to the right. The first is in Amsterdam's Van Gogh Museum, the second is located at the Art Institute of Chicago, and the third is in Paris's Musée d'Orsay.

Keep Score: 13 Changes ☐ ☐ ☐ ☐ ☐ ☐ ☐ ☐ ☐ ☐ ☐ ☐ ☐

Martin Johnson Heade
Two Hummingbirds Above a White Orchid (c. 1875–90)

Born in Bucks County, Pennsylvania, Heade was the son of a farmer and most likely learned to paint from his neighbor, the folk artist Edward Hicks.

Heade was fascinated by hummingbirds and painted a series of approximately forty-five 10 x 12-inch paintings using these birds as the subject. Many, like the one seen here, were combined with images of lush, tropical flowers like the orchid.

During his lifetime, Heade was practically unknown, and he was nearly forgotten altogether after his death in 1904. Rediscovered in the 1940s, he is now regarded as one of the greatest American Romantic painters.

Heade worked with very large canvases...one of his landscape paintings measured $4\frac{1}{2}$ feet x $7\frac{1}{2}$ feet!

Keep Score:
7 Changes

☐ ☐ ☐ ☐
☐ ☐ ☐

Hans Holbein the Younger
Henry VIII (1539–40)

There are 80 Holbein portrait drawings at Windsor Castle.

Holbein's paintings were admired for the details of the texture and design of his subject's clothing rather than for facial expressions.

ANNO · ÆTATIS ·   SVÆ · XLIX ·

· ANNO · ETATIS ·   · SVÆ · XXIX ·

The rich colors of the jewels and the detailed fabric in this painting emphasize the king's wealth and power.

Keep Score:
8 Changes

☐ ☐ ☐ ☐
☐ ☐ ☐ ☐

Winslow Homer
Snap the Whip (1872)

The boys in this picture are playing Snap the Whip, a recess game also known as Crack the Whip. To play, children hold hands in a long line and then run fast. The first ones in line stop suddenly, yanking the other kids sideways and causing the ones on the other end to break the chain and fall.

Homer loved to create pictures of "common folk" that told a story. These stories were often based on his own experiences and observations.

This painting was displayed at the 1876 Centennial Exposition in Philadelphia, Pennsylvania.

Neither sneakers nor zippers had been invented when this picture was painted. The boys are probably trying to save wear and tear on their leather shoes by playing barefoot. Suspenders and buttons are holding up their pants.

In his later years, Homer settled on the coast of Maine, where he built a studio and began to paint pictures that showed the beauty and power of the ocean.

Keep Score: 10 Changes ☐ ☐ ☐ ☐ ☐ ☐ ☐ ☐ ☐ ☐

Leonardo da Vinci
Mona Lisa (1506)

The *Mona Lisa* is probably the most famous painting in the world and is the top attraction at the Louvre Museum in Paris, France. It is seen by millions of visitors yearly.

The popularity of the painting is largely due to the fact that it was stolen from the Louvre Museum in 1911. The theft created lots of publicity before the painting was recovered two years later.

Although her true identity remains a mystery, most historians believe Mona Lisa to be the wife of 16th-century Florentine businessman Francesco del Giocondo, who is thought to have commissioned the portrait. This would also explain the painting's other titles, *La Gioconda* (in Italian) and *La Joconde* (in French).

The painting is encased in a glass bulletproof box and kept at a constant 68 degrees Fahrenheit and 55 percent humidity. Once a year, the box is opened and the painting gets a "check-up."

Da Vinci never sold this painting and legend has it that when he lay dying, the *Mona Lisa* was at his bedside.

Keep Score:
9 Changes

☐ ☐ ☐ ☐ ☐
☐ ☐ ☐ ☐

Emanuel Leutze
Washington Crossing the Delaware (1851) (Detail)

This painting shows the historic moment when General George Washington led the American revolutionary troops across the Delaware River in order to surprise the English and Hessian troops in the Battle of Trenton. It took place the day after Christmas in 1776.

The design on the New Jersey quarter, the third coin in the 50 State Quarters Program, is based on this painting.

In reality, there is no way that Washington could have stood up for this journey without falling into the freezing water.

This famous work was actually painted in Germany, where the artist used the Rhine River as a model for the Delaware. He also changed the setting to daytime, although the actual battle took place about 3 a.m., in the dark.

The flag shown behind Washington's head didn't exist at the time of the event pictured here. The "Stars and Stripes" shown in the painting didn't replace the Grand Union Flag until six months after this battle took place.

The original painting is more than 12 feet high and 21 feet long!

Keep Score: 9 Changes ☐ ☐ ☐ ☐ ☐ ☐ ☐ ☐ ☐

Édouard Manet
A Bar at the Folies-Bergère (1881–82)

The Folies-Bergère was one of the most elaborate variety-show halls in Paris, with entertainment ranging from ballets to circus acts. Can you find the trapeze artist?

Manet included his signature on the wine bottle at bottom left, "Manet/1882."

Manet painted scenes and people from everyday life in a realistic and natural manner, as close as possible to the way they actually looked. Because of this approach, he is often described as a Realist.

Manet spent time with the Impressionists, although he never exhibited with them. Some of his later paintings are very "impressionistic" in style. This painting is a visual puzzle that has sparked debate for over 100 years!

The woman standing behind the marble counter appears to be lost in thought. But in the reflection in the mirror behind her, she appears to be waiting on a customer.

Keep Score: 10 Changes ☐ ☐ ☐ ☐ ☐ ☐ ☐ ☐ ☐ ☐

Jean-François Millet
The Gleaners (1857)

This painting was the first of many rural scenes that were based on Millet's own childhood memories. He was famous for portraying the gravity, hardship, and dignity of common laborers in a way that made them almost heroic figures.

Millet is quoted as saying "the human side of art is what touches me most."

Millet has illustrated the three phases of this difficult, backbreaking, repetitive job: bending over, picking the crop, and straightening up again.

This work is the result of ten years of research on the subject of gleaners. The women represent the rural working class, told to go quickly through the fields at sunset to pick up the stray grains missed by the harvesters.

Claude Monet
La Japonaise (1876)
(Camille Monet in Japanese Costume)

Though he never went to Japan, Monet was fascinated with the country and its art. He owned 231 Japanese prints that greatly influenced his own painting.

The woman in this painting is Monet's first wife, Camille.

When he moved to Giverny in 1883, Monet built a Japanese garden that included a curved wooden bridge and a pond for his favorite flower: water lilies. During the latter part of his life, he painted these lilies hundreds of times in every type of light and in every season.

The term "Impressionism" came from the name of one of Monet's paintings, *Impression: Sunrise*, and defined a style of painting.

Usually Claude Monet loved to paint outdoors. He was constantly amazed by the way light could change a scene.

Keep Score:
8 Changes

☐ ☐ ☐ ☐
☐ ☐ ☐ ☐

Rembrandt van Rijn
The Night Watch (1642)
(Detail)

This is the most famous painting in Amsterdam's Rijksmuseum, where it was installed in 1817 and moved to a specially designed gallery in 1906. The painting has only been moved once from this location and that was during World War II, when it was rolled up and stored in a bunker.

The painting actually has another title, *The Company of Frans Banning Cocq and Willem van Ruytenburch.*

Eighteen soldiers paid to be included in this painting. Rembrandt added others to make the scene livelier. Three people on the left side of the picture disappeared in the 18th century when part of the canvas was cut off.

Rembrandt painted his wife Saskia's features on the little girl who appears in the front of the painting. He painted himself as well. He appears in the back of the painting, the lower half of his face hidden by the outstretched arm of the Sergeant.

It's not certain where Rembrandt painted this masterpiece, but some evidence suggests it was done in the backyard of his home because it was too big to lean against a wall in any of the rooms inside the house.

Keep Score: 8 Changes ☐ ☐ ☐ ☐ ☐ ☐ ☐ ☐

Frederic Remington
A Dash for the Timber (1889) (Detail)

This painting launched Remington's career as a major artist after it was exhibited at the National Academy in 1889.

While attending Yale, Remington drew journalistic cartoons for the university's paper.

Remington produced over 3,000 drawings and paintings in his short lifetime (he died at the age of 48).

In addition to paintings, Remington enjoyed creating three-dimensional works of art. He completed 22 bronze sculptures of cowboys and other western scenes.

The artist left college in order to travel across the U.S. on horseback. During the journey, he worked as a cowboy and prospected for gold, all the while filling a diary with observations and collecting artifacts that he would later use in his paintings.

Remington was a painter, sculptor, and writer.

Keep Score: 9 Changes ☐ ☐ ☐ ☐ ☐ ☐ ☐ ☐ ☐

Pierre-Auguste Renoir
Girls at the Piano (1892)

Renoir took his time to develop and refine this scene in a series of five canvases. There is a nearly identical version of this painting that still exists. (It was once in the collection of Renoir's fellow Impressionist, Gustave Caillebotte.)

Renoir began his artistic career in his early teens painting designs on china in a Paris porcelain factory.

During the last 20 years of his life, Renoir was so crippled with arthritis that he found it difficult to paint. By strapping a brush to his hand, he was able to continue doing what he loved.

Renoir was inspired to become an artist after a visit to the Louvre in Paris when he was about nine years old. Before he died, he was able to visit the museum and see his own paintings hanging there!

Keep Score:
9 Changes

☐ ☐ ☐ ☐ ☐
☐ ☐ ☐ ☐

Henri Rousseau
Woman Walking in an Exotic Forest (1905)

Rousseau did not begin to paint until he was almost 40 years old. He was an untrained, completely self-taught artist.

He is best known for his exotic jungle scenes. Visits to the zoos and the botanical gardens in Paris provided inspiration for his imaginative art.

Rousseau held a job with the Paris Customs office when he took up painting as a hobby. He retired from his job early, at age 49, so that he could devote his time entirely to art.

There are more than twenty jungle paintings, almost all of which are large in size.

Keep Score:
6 Changes

☐ ☐ ☐ ☐
☐ ☐

Georges Seurat
Bathers at Asnières (1883–84)

Asnières is an industrial suburb west of Paris on the River Seine. This painting shows a group of young workmen relaxing by the river.

Considered one of the most important Post-Impressionist painters, Seurat was known for his extraordinary attention to detail.

Seurat invented a technique of applying small dots, or points, of color to a canvas in order to create variations of shade without losing any of the color's brilliance. Today, this technique is known as Pointillism.

While this particular painting was not done using his Pointillist technique (which he had not yet invented), Seurat later reworked areas of the picture using dots of contrasting color to create a brighter, more luminous effect.

Seurat completed seven very large paintings and about 500 smaller ones during his brief lifetime. He was only 31 years old when he died.

Keep Score: 11 Changes ☐ ☐ ☐ ☐ ☐ ☐ ☐ ☐ ☐ ☐ ☐

Johannes Vermeer
Woman Holding a Balance (c. 1664)

Vermeer only painted about 40 pictures during his lifetime.

Vermeer had 15 children with his wife Catherina. Eleven of them lived to grow into adulthood.

Vermeer usually included only one or two people in his pictures and most of his paintings were set indoors.

His works usually have a window at the left of the picture.

Keep Score:
9 Changes
❑ ❑ ❑ ❑ ❑
❑ ❑ ❑ ❑

Pages 4–5 Ambrosius Bosschaert
Bouquet of Flowers on a Ledge

- Moth Added
- Butterfly Removed
- Flower Color Changed
- Leaf Removed
- Eiffel Tower Added

- Spider Removed
- Ribbon Added
- Shell Added
- Fish Added
- Flower Added

Pages 6–7 Pieter Bruegel the Elder
Hunters in the Snow

- Bird's Nest Added
- Sign Straightened
- Window Removed
- Large Dog Removed
- Small Dog Removed
- Ice Skates Added
- Hunter Removed

- Chimney Added
- Bridge Arch Removed
- Woman Added
- Skater Removed
- Skater Added
- Mountain Added
- Bird Added

Pages 8–9 Gustave Caillebotte
Rue de Paris

- Building Raised
- Man Removed
- Horseman Added
- Umbrella Color Changed
- Newspaper Added
- Dog Added

- Vest Color Changed
- Purse Added
- Pipe Added
- Window Added
- Light Bulb Added

Pages 10–11   Vittore Carpaccio
Young Knight in a Landscape

- Bird Removed
- Sign Added
- Wizard Added
- Peacock Reversed
- Shield Added
- Horse's Leg Straightened
- Flower Added

- Weasel Removed
- Rock Added
- Dog Removed
- Stripes Removed from Sword
- Hair Shortened
- Bird Removed
- Squirrel Added

Pages 12–13   Mary Cassatt
In the Loge

- Man Added
- Earring Changed
- Collar Removed
- Woman Removed

- Handrail Color Changed
- Fan Changed
- Chocolates Added

Pages 14–15   Paul Cézanne
Still Life with Apples

- Cézanne's *Man in a Blue Smock* Added
- Apple Added
- Pineapple Added
- Lemon Added

- Stripe Added
- Flower Design on Jar Removed
- Apple Color Changed
- Bottle Color Changed

Pages 16–17   Edgar Degas
The Dance Class

- Bubblegum Added
- Dog Removed
- Music Stand Added
- Roller Skate Added
- Cane Removed
- Ribbon Color Changed
- Wall Color Changed
- Pillar Added

Pages 18–19   Albrecht Dürer
Self-Portrait

- Hair Removed
- Tassel Removed
- Ribbon Added
- Stripe on Sleeve Added
- Thumb Removed
- Writing Under Window Removed
- Donuts Added
- Scene Outside Window Changed

Pages 20–21   Jan van Eyck
The Arnolfini Portrait

- Candle Added
- Moth Added
- Fruit Removed
- Shoe Removed
- Starfish Added
- Dog Changed to Rabbit
- Pillow Color Changed
- Sleeve Color Changed
- Pattern Added to Pillow
- Mirror Changed to Clock
- Writing Removed from Wall

Pages 28–29 Hans Holbein the Younger
Henry VIII

- Hat Decoration Turned
- Eyebrows Darkened
- Beard Filled in
- Locket Changed to Watch
- Gloves Color Changed
- Ring Moved
- Sleeve Decoration Removed
- Date Changed

Pages 30–31 Winslow Homer
Snap the Whip

- Water Tower Added
- Ball Cap Added
- Boy Removed
- Rock Added
- Pants Color Changed
- Door Added
- Suspender Removed
- Boy Removed
- Tree Added
- Smoke Added

Pages 32–33 Leonardo da Vinci
Mona Lisa

- Boat Added
- Road Reversed
- Flower Added
- Ring Added
- Necklace Added
- Lipstick Added
- Eyes Reversed
- Trees Added
- Bird Added

Pages 34–35 Emanuel Leutze
Washington Crossing the Delaware
(detail)

- Lighthouse Added
- Sailboat Added
- Leg Moved
- Sword Removed
- Rubber Duck Added
- Sash Color Changed
- Man Removed
- Star Removed
- Tassels Removed

Pages 36–37 Édouard Manet
A Bar at the Folies-Bergère

- Gloves Color Changed
- Bottle Added
- Bottle Removed
- Bracelet Added
- Flower Added
- Apple Added
- Label Removed
- Necklace Color Changed
- Bow Added
- Light Added

Pages 38–39 Jean-François Millet
The Gleaners

- Sky Color Changed
- Haystack Added
- Headscarf Color Changed
- Gopher Added
- Shovel Added
- Pattern Added to Skirt
- Hand Removed
- Flowers Added
- Horseman Removed

Pages 46–47   Pierre-Auguste Renoir
Girls at the Piano

- Painting Removed
- Bow Removed
- Sleeve Longer
- Sheet of Paper Added
- Flute Added
- Candle Added
- Pattern Changed on Vase
- Wall Color Changed
- Lace Collar Removed

Pages 48–49   Henri Rousseau
Woman Walking in an Exotic Forest

- Orange Removed
- Flower Color Changed
- Leaf Removed
- Skirt Color Changed
- Lion Added
- Tree Limb Added

Pages 50–51   Georges Seurat
Bathers at Asnières

- Tree Added
- Umbrella Added
- Stripe Added to Hat
- Dog's Head Turned
- Books Added
- Swimmer Removed

- Hat Color Changed
- Building Taller
- Boat Removed
- Smoke Added
- Hot Air Balloon Added

Pages 52–53   Johannes Vermeer
Woman Holding a Balance

- Vermeer's *Girl with a Pearl Earring* Added
- Horseshoe Added
- Crown Added
- Jewelry Removed
- Tea Bag Added

- Cup and Saucer Added
- Pattern Added to Skirt
- Dog Added
- Painting Changed to Rembrandt's *The Storm on the Sea of Galilee*

Index